THE
CELESTINE PROPHECY:

A POCKET GUIDE
TO THE NINE INSIGHTS

W9-BSZ-145

James Redfield

WARNER **W** TREASURES
PUBLISHED BY WARNER BOOKS
A TIME WARNER COMPANY

FOR MY DAUGHTERS
MEGAN AND KELLY

❧

Warner Treasures is a trademark of
Warner Books, Inc.,
1271 Avenue of the Americas,
New York, NY 10020

Visit our Web site at
http://pathfinder.com/twep

Ⓦ A Time Warner Company
Printed in China

First Printing: September 1996
10 9 8 7 6 5 4

ISBN: 0-446-91206-9

Book design by Lisa C. McGarry

Now the essence of *The Celestine Prophecy* can be with you always. In this special pocket edition of one of the most beloved spiritual guides ever published, author James Redfield defines and concisely explains each of the Nine Insights of *The Celestine Prophecy*. A little book that you can carry everywhere and study at your convenience, it is a perfect way to keep in touch with our changing world and your unfolding adventure.

Introduction

Self-published in 1993, and by Warner Books in 1994, *The Celestine Prophecy* has enjoyed remarkable popularity, having sold more than 3 million copies in North America and winning translation in over 30 languages. Surprisingly, most of this readership has been built not from media publicity, but from word-of-mouth referrals, as readers who loved the book took the time to recommend it to others.

Naturally, I'm often asked about the meaning of this success. What accounts for the phenomenon? What is the spirit of this book? I must admit that to some extent I remain as mystified as others. I wrote the book to be a parable about the search for spirituality in our time, an adventure that weaved together personal experience with ideas about the new spiritual renaissance slowly emerging on our planet. I felt that this "new awareness" was manifesting through what amounted to mass "Insights" or "revelations" moving through human culture.

I believe now that these "Insights" are in fact archetypal, built into the structure of our psychology and our need for spiritual understanding. The story in *The Celestine Prophecy* is meaningful because we can identify with the perceptions and inner shifts experienced by the characters in the book. It seems to communicate a view of life that we inherently recognize. In other words, the insights seem familiar because they're coming to all of us at the same time.

The essays appearing in this book review and discuss each of the nine Insights of *The Celestine Prophecy*. Nothing seems more fitting than to survey the "Celestine phenomenon" and ponder where it might be taking us.

The First Insight:

A
CRITICAL
MASS

A new spiritual awakening is occurring in human culture, an awakening brought about by a critical mass of individuals who experience their lives as a spiritual unfolding, a journey in which we are led forward by mysterious coincidences.

The First Insight is the insight of awakening, and focuses on the mysterious coincidences that occur in each of our lives. Of course, for centuries, we have been discounting such occurrences as pure chance and thus without meaning. But as we ponder the spiritual dimension of our existence, opening our minds, we begin to experience phenomena that cannot be dismissed and pushed away. Why, for instance, do we wake up one morning thinking of an old friend only to get a call from this very person later in the day? Why does a casual meeting with a certain person at a certain time often lead to great advance in our careers, our relationships, our awareness of inner talent?

The Swiss psychologist Carl Jung called this phenomenon *synchronicity*, the perception of meaningful life coincidences, and we cannot stop and ponder these occurrences without beginning to see direct evidence of a divine force involved in our lives. We are not here in this life merely by accident, playing out a meaningless drama. Our lives have purpose, a sense of destiny. We seem to be guided forward by a mysterious providence.

Such synchronicity is easy to see in retrospect, as we look back to the fateful twists of our pasts: the family experience that shaped us, the people who influenced our early interests and educational choices, the forks in the road that led us to where we are today.

Much harder is to keep this awareness fully operative in the present. Whom will we meet today? What information might arrive that will shape our life direction?

We immediately want to understand more about the process and more about where these mysterious coincidences are taking us. We even ask: Are they real? Is our perception of synchronicity really important? Such questions immediately lead us to the Second Insight.

The Second Insight:

THE
LONGER
NOW

Our new spiritual awakening represents the creation of a more complete worldview, which replaces a five-hundred-year-old preoccupation with secular survival and comfort. While this preoccupation with technological advancement was an important step, our awakening to life's coincidences is opening us up to the real purpose of human life on this planet and the real nature of our universe.

The Second Insight occurs when we grasp the historical importance of our awakening. We now see that we have existed in a secular slumber for centuries and that the awareness of "Celestine moments" in our lives represents an awakening from what has been a preoccupation with material security and comfort.

The European Renaissance began when we lost faith in the ability of medieval churchmen to describe our spiritual reality. We created a mandate for science to investigate the world around us and to discover our spiritual nature. Until recently, scientists focused solely on discovering the forces thought to be governing our world.

But the loss of certainty brought on by the fall of the churchmen created a deep existential insecurity. What was the real purpose of human life? We eased our insecurity by preoccupying ourselves with another goal: physical progress. We decided to settle into this Earth of ours, improving our conditions in the physical world—at least until we learned our true spiritual situation.

During the Industrial Revolution, we saw major technological gains, reaffirming the mind-set of "progress." Our need for spiritual knowledge was almost lost. Preoccupying ourselves with secular concerns, we accepted the illusion that we lived in a rational and predictable universe, where chance occurrences had no meaning.

In the last decades of our century, led by science itself, this worldview, devoid of spiritual mystery, began to disintegrate. We grasp the Second Insight when we understand the historical momentum leading us to a new, more mysterious, more spiritual life view.

The Third Insight:

A
MATTER OF
ENERGY

We now experience that we live not in a material universe, but in a universe of dynamic energy. Everything extant is a field of sacred energy that we can sense and intuit. Moreover, we humans can project our energy by focusing our attention in the desired direction (where attention goes, energy flows), influencing other energy systems and increasing the pace of coincidences in our lives.

The work of Albert Einstein in the early twentieth century sounded the death knell for the old, secular worldview. Since the mid-eighteenth century, science had viewed our universe according to Isaac Newton's mechanistic theories. According to Newton, matter and the atoms of which it is composed were solid material, interacting according to immutable natural laws.

Newton held that we lived in a clockwork universe precisely held together. Every action in this universe was thought to be the result of a discernible physical cause, like billiard balls bouncing off each other in a predictable, orderly way. Galaxies, stars, planets, all remained in orderly motion through the force of gravity, a pull that kept heavenly bodies circling other larger bodies. Newtonian ideas led to the illusion that the universe is devoid of mystery.

Then, with a series of startling insights, Einstein turned our world upside down. He showed that matter isn't ultimately solid. It is in fact shaped and compressed energy. Einstein's other discoveries were equally transformative. Time is not constant, but relative to the mass or speed of a particular object. Other research in physics has discovered particles that appear in two places at the same time or disappear and reappear in places totally inaccessible under the laws of the Newtonian worldview.

Slowly, we are opening to the true mystery of this universe. We live in a universe of dynamic fields of energy, a dynamic universe that includes ourselves. We are intricate energy systems, fields transcending our physical bodies and reaching out to touch and influence other energy systems.

The Fourth Insight:

THE
STRUGGLE FOR
POWER

Too often humans cut themselves off from the greater source of our energy systems and so feel weak and insecure. To gain energy, we tend to manipulate or force others to give us attention and thus energy. When we successfully dominate others in this way, we feel more powerful, but they are left weakened and often fight back. Competition for scarce human energy is the cause of all conflict between people.

The great contribution of psychologists in our time—Carl Jung, Otto Rank, Norman O. Brown, and Eric

Berne—has been to show that humans tend to be motivated by deep insecurity. We feel alone and search for the security derived from being validated by others. We want to feel that others approve of and even defer to our knowledge and position. We try to subtly force this validation by controlling the thoughts and opinions of those around us.

Looked at experientially, we recognize the feeling. Alone, we often feel anxious, our thoughts cloudy, sensing uncertainty about our worth or status. But when we're with someone who is paying attention, listening to what we have to say with deference, we feel empowered, ever buoyant. Thoughts seem to flow easily and we reach a sense of clarity about who we are. This is the feeling that entices and motivates us. From early childhood, we learn ways to interact, beguiling and forcing others to defer to our opinions.

All of us have also experienced another person *seeking to understand our sense of who we are* or what we know, in order to confuse us into deferring to that person. When we try to resist this sense of being invalidated or undermined, disagreements, often difficult to resolve, arise.

This negative interaction is common in human affairs, but we are beginning to understand this interaction in terms of energy dynamics. When we force someone else to defer to us, we actually suck energy from the energy field of the other person in order to produce an energy boost in ourselves. But we now know that we need not resort to stealing additional energy from others. We have at our disposal another source, a divine source of spiritual energy, for our ultimate security.

The Fifth Insight:

THE
MESSAGE OF THE
MYSTICS

Insecurity and violence end when we experience a connection with divine energy within, a connection described by mystics of all traditions. A sense of lightness—buoyancy—and the constant sensation of love are measures of this connection. If these measures are present, the connection is real. If not, it is only pretended.

Every religion has had its share of mystical thinkers who have looked beyond the dogma of the religion to explore its inner experiential truth. These mystics have one common message: each of us has access to a connection with the energy of the Divine. We must make a conscious choice to be open to this connection, a choice deeply conceived and wholly felt.

Mystics describe the nature of this connecting experience, giving us several precise measures by which to judge our own attempts. First, the mystics describe a sense of buoyancy, the feeling of being suddenly "light on one's feet." Some mystics reportedly even levitated during these ecstatic states.

Another measure is a sense of euphoria, joy, and peace—peace that is independent of one's own particular life situation but that liberates the soul from any attachments to outcomes. Thus freed, one acts and creates according to conscience.

Lastly, the sensation of love is the most often described attribute of a true inner connection with the Divine. This experience is not merely telling oneself that one is or should be "loving." It is an actual experience of a state of love. Perhaps this experience is misunderstood because we have been used to thinking that love needs an object. We love a spouse, a child, a parent, or even an activity. But the mystical sense of love is love without an object. It is love as a constant communion with God.

These measures tell us whether we are opening up to the energy available to us from within. Once this connection is experienced, it is unmistakable. We begin to gain strength and energy, not from the deference and attention coming from others, but from our own growing inner source that leads us in search of our spiritual mission.

The Sixth Insight:

CLEARING
THE PAST

The more we stay connected, the more we are actually aware of those times when we lose connection, usually when we are under stress. In these times, we can see our own particular way of stealing energy from others. Once our manipulations are brought to personal awareness, our connection becomes more constant and we can discover our own growth path in life and our spiritual mission—the personal way we can contribute to the world.

Once we find our own experience of an inner source of divine energy, we become acutely aware of those times when we lose this connection. Usually, we realize that this loss of connection occurs during times of stress when we feel particularly anxious and think we have to seize control of the interactions of our lives.

It is at these times and under these circumstances that we can detect the particular style in which we attempt to control others, one or more of what I have described as "control dramas." These styles of controlling fall along a spectrum from passive to aggressive. For instance, if we seek to control another by making that person feel guilty for not doing enough for us (gaining energy when he or she buys into this "guilt trip" and begins to attend to us), we can be described as a "poor-me."

If, on the other hand, we seek to control others in a slightly less passive way by remaining detached, secretive, and vague—hoping to entice someone into chasing us around in order to probe and figure us out, and thus gaining energy from that person's attention in that manner—then we are acting "aloof."

More aggressive behavior would be

the attempt to control others by "find-ing fault" and making others feel self-conscious and monitored, a style designated as that of the "interrogator." Lastly, we come to the most aggressive control drama of all, "intimidator," who wins energy by frightening others into paying attention.

If we are to avoid falling into these control dramas, each of us must first identify our particular "drama," or in the case of multiple use, dramas, and become fully conscious of these manipulations every time we employ them. Why? Because any unconscious habit brought fully into awareness is released, and we can begin to lengthen those periods when we are in a state of connection, trust, and love—opening us up to our real purpose in life, our spiritual mission.

Once we bring our control drama into awareness and stay connected with our inner source of energy, we are free to look at ourselves and our lives in a more truthful way. First we can see how the dynamics in our early family reinforced our control drama and animated the power struggles with family members. Then we can move beyond these struggles to see the spiritual purpose behind our early family experience.

We must step back and ask: Why was I there? What life issues was I meant to be sensitized to? To explore this question, we must look at both our parents in terms of their lifestyles. What we might ask is: What did my father stand for? What were his strengths and accomplishments? What did he want from life that he never attained?

Similarly, we must look at our mother's life and ask the very same questions about her. What was her life about? What was she trying to establish in the world, regardless of how successfully?

Out of this analysis we can see a momentum into which we were born, two points of view that we wanted to integrate into our early lives. Looked at spiritually, we can see two approaches to life that were to some extent different, perhaps even contrary. Yet we were placed there precisely to resolve and synthesize their truths into a higher form.

This is the spiritual process through which one generation evolves the reality it inherits into another, more truthful form. Our whole lives are about finding the combined truth of our early family and then continually evolving this truth into higher and higher form until the telling of it becomes our mission. Once we understand this truth, we can see that all the experiences, the synchronicity, of our lives were a preparation for this mission. It becomes our way of uplifting the world.

The Seventh Insight:

ENGAGING
THE FLOW

Knowing our personal mission further enhances the flow of mysterious coincidences as we are guided toward our destinies. First we have a question; then dreams, daydreams, and intuitions lead us toward the answers, which usually are synchronistically provided by the wisdom of another human being.

Once we discover the "truth" we tell—our message about what is important in living life—the mysterious coincidence, the synchronicity, really increases in our lives. For some of us, the discovery of our mission will perhaps lead us to change our jobs. Others will find that we are in exactly the right place to tell our truth. Still others might stay in an incompatible job but pursue their mission as an avocation. But on whatever stage we find ourselves, we will see that the synchronicity in our lives pertains to the pursuit of the mission.

We begin to see more clearly how the mysterious coincidences happen. It begins with an intuition, a hunch, a mental image of saying something to someone, of going somewhere initiating a project. Sometimes we don't quite see the full picture. But when we act on the hunch, when other events begin to take place that feel destined, we begin to see why we were intuitively guided to make the move. Each event brings other intuitions, and we are shown where to go to tell our truth, which groups need our message, and what form of communication to use.

Dreams are especially valuable when determining our path. Dreams always contain the characteristics of stories: plot, characters, action. No matter how strange the dream, we can analyze the plot. What are the characters saying? What emotions are being expressed? What are they seeking? From whom are they fleeing? Take the plot of the dream and superimpose it on the plot of your life. What are the similarities? Is there similar action happening in your life of which you may have been unaware? Is the action in the dream something you may want to try? Or is the dream telling you to avoid this action at all cost?

We must be ever alert for messages.

The Eighth Insight:

THE
INTERPERSONAL
ETHIC

We can increase the frequency of guiding coincidences by uplifting every person who comes into our lives. Care must be taken not to lose our inner connection in romantic relationships. Uplifting others is especially effective in groups where each member can feel the energy of all the others. With children it is extremely important for their early security and growth. By seeing the beauty in every face, we lift others into their wisest self and increase the chances of hearing a synchronistic message.

As our perception of life coincidences leads us toward the accomplishment of our missions, we begin to notice that most synchronistic messages come from other human beings. When we receive just the right information at just the right time, most often it comes to us via the words or writing of another, sometimes in the most unlikely of circumstances.

But the question arises: How many of these coincidental encounters do we still miss simply because we are too shy to follow up on a friendly stranger's remark, or to make that first gesture of conversation ourselves? We are learning to watch for even the slightest possibility of a coincidental message because we know it could come from anyone.

And more than that, we are learning that with the strength of our attention we can uplift those with whom we cross paths, actually sending energy their way so that they feel suddenly insightful, able to see their lives and ideas with a higher clarity, and so perhaps give us an important truth. The technique for this act of "uplifting" is to focus on the other person's face in a special way. Somehow we are able to see the higher self, the inspired personality, the Divine, in the face of another.

This interpersonal ethic can also be applied to interaction within a group. When each member of a group uplifts whoever happens to be speaking, remarkable levels of energy and insight can be achieved. Likewise, when operating under this insight, parenting, teaching, and romantic involvement all take on a higher spiritual meaning. As humankind begins to interact in a conscious spiritual manner, human culture will begin to accelerate into a completely spiritual form.

The Ninth Insight:

THE
EMERGING
CULTURE

As we all evolve toward the best completion of our spiritual missions, the technological means of survival will be fully automated as humans focus instead on synchronistic growth. Such growth will move humans into ever-higher energy states, ultimately transforming our bodies into spiritual form and uniting this dimension of existence with the afterlife dimension, ending the cycle of birth and death.

Learning to stay connected to divine energy within and actively pursuing a sense of spiritual mission, human culture will continue to transform. The Ninth Insight is the awareness of how our culture is evolving.

Experts predict that in the twenty-first century, culture will be changing so fast that we will shift jobs, and maybe whole careers, many times during a typical lifetime. And because of computers and other technological advances, we will live in an age of information, leaving the industrial age behind. We will shift our focus from making the products necessary to our civilization to rapidly knowing what to make, when to make it, and how to make it faster.

As we continue to evolve spiritually, we will embrace an increasing automation of the basic means of subsistence and will focus individually on our spiritual purpose. Listening to our intuition, we will learn to be in the right place at the right time in order to provide our unique truth to others. We will compensate those who provide us with synchronistic information. As this automation is completed, the spiritual process of giving will become the dominant structure of economic life.

Life will then be focused completely on personal evolution, led by synchronistic interaction with others. As we achieve increasingly higher energy levels through this "interpersonal ethic," our bodily state will continue to increase in vibration until we become purely spiritual beings, here on planet Earth. As this occurs, we will live not just in the physical dimension but in the afterlife dimension as well. In this way, the two dimensions unite as one, ending the cycle of birth and death.

IMAGING THE FUTURE

The kind of future humans will create is our choice. We can embrace our inherent spirituality and find purpose in discovering who we are and where we can go, or we can encapsulate ourselves in a vision of fear.

Scientists warn us every day that human society cannot continue on its present, unenlightened course, that our habitual way of doing things will ultimately overpopulate the planet, destroy our natural ecosystems, poison our bodies, and catastrophically alter our weather patterns. Science is predicting a cycle of massive earthquakes and increased volcanic activity. At the same time, economic disruptions and limited government budgets would seem to indicate increased violence and crime and alienation.

But at the same time, underneath this expectation of the worst is a growing number of people who understand the spiritual alternative. In a sense, a dramatic polarization of opinion is taking place, and the question is clear: Will we resign ourselves to the apocalyptic scenario of the future and retreat further into thinking only of our short-term self-interest, or will we consciously embrace and cocreate a future of love and spiritual purpose? My own sense is that we're approaching the great divide, and the heroes are all in place.

INFORMATION
FROM THE AUTHOR

A monthly newsletter is available from the author on the ideas brought forth in *The Celestine Prophecy* and *The Tenth Insight*. "The Celestine Journal" chronicles the author's present experiences and reflections on the spiritual renaissance occurring on our planet. Subscription rates are $29.95 for one year from Sartori Publishing, P.O. Box 360988, Hoover, Alabama 35236.

Warner Books is not responsible for the delivery or content of the information or materials provided by the author. The reader should address any questions to the author at the above address.